MID-AUTUMN FESTIVAL

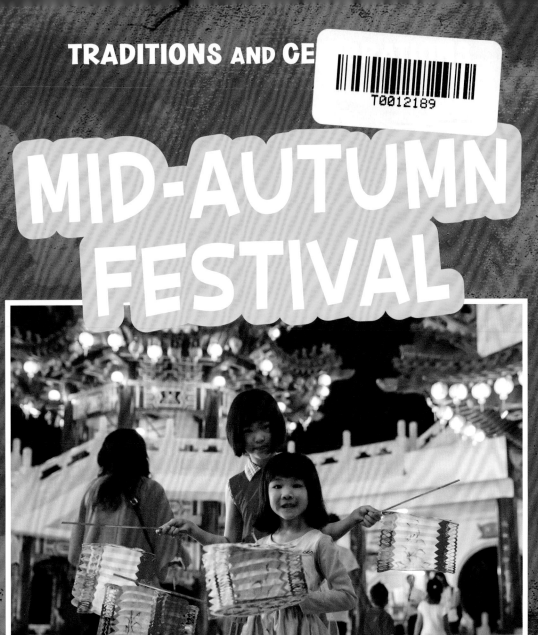

by Ailynn Collins

PEBBLE
a capstone imprint

Published by Pebble, an imprint of Capstone
1710 Roe Crest Drive, North Mankato, Minnesota 56003
capstonepub.com

Library of Congress Cataloging-in-Publication Data
Names: Collins, Ailynn, 1964- author.
Title: Mid-autumn festival / by Ailynn Collins.
Description: North Mankato, Minnesota : Pebble, 2024. | Series: Traditions and celebrations | Includes bibliographical references and index. | Audience: Ages 5 to 8 | Audience: Grades 2–3 | Summary: "The Mid-Autumn Festival is a traditional holiday celebrated in Chinese culture. Also called the Moon Festival or Mooncake Festival, this celebration is all about appreciating the moon and the harvest. Although the date of the festival changes each year, it always falls around the time of the harvest moon. From family gatherings to paper lanterns to eating mooncakes, different Asian countries have different celebrations. Learn how people honor this special day in countries and cultures around the world."—Provided by publisher.
Identifiers: LCCN 2022050147 (print) | LCCN 2022050148 (ebook) | ISBN 9780756575731 (hardcover) | ISBN 9780756575687 (paperback) | ISBN 9780756575694 (pdf) | ISBN 9780756575717 (kindle edition) | ISBN 9780756575724 (epub)
Subjects: LCSH: Mid-autumn Festival—Juvenile literature. | China—Social life and customs—Juvenile literature.
Classification: LCC GT4502.7 .C65 2024 (print) | LCC GT4502.7 (ebook) | DDC 394.264—dc23/eng/20230109
LC record available at https://lccn.loc.gov/2022050147
LC ebook record available at https://lccn.loc.gov/2022050148

Editorial Credits
Editor: Alison Deering; Designer: Jaime Willems; Media Researcher: Rebekah Hubstenberger; Production Specialist: Whitney Schaefer

Image Credits
Associated Press: Ahn Young-joon, 19, Hau Dinh, 28; Getty Images: Edwin Tan, 11, Fuse, 22, Images By Tang Ming Tung, 25, Wang Yukun, 15, zyxeos30, 14; Shutterstock: AlexanderLS, 7, Chananchida Ch, 23, Elena Ermakova, 1, huntergol hp, 26, Kobby Dagan, 21, Lukas Kurka, 12, Manintino, 5, Michael Urmann, 16, SvetlanaSF, cover, TOMO, 18, Vietnam Stock Images, 27, 29, Vitanine, 13, yienkeat, 8

Design Elements
Shutterstock: Rafal Kulik

All internet sites appearing in back matter were available and accurate when this book was sent to press.

Printed and bound in China. P0SS79

TABLE OF CONTENTS

Words in **bold** are in the glossary.

WHAT IS THE MID-AUTUMN FESTIVAL?

Children carrying pretty paper lanterns. Families looking at the full moon. People eating mooncakes and fruit. This is the Mid-Autumn Festival.

The Mid-Autumn Festival is a Chinese holiday. But it is celebrated by Asian people all over the world. It is also called the Moon, or Mooncake, Festival.

Different **legends** tell how this day became a holiday. The most common one is about the Lady in the Moon.

Long ago, there were 10 suns in the sky. They made life very hard. Crops dried up. People and animals were hot and thirsty.

A great **archer** shot down nine of the suns with his bow and arrow. The people were very thankful. The gods gave the archer a special gift. It was a **potion** that would make him live forever.

The archer takes aim at the many suns.

Chang'e floats up to the moon.

The archer was married to a very beautiful woman. Her name was Chang'e (Chung-ur). The archer loved his wife very much. He didn't want to live forever without her. They kept the potion safe in their house.

One night, Chang'e was alone at home. A man broke in. He wanted to steal the potion. Chang'e didn't want it to end up in the wrong hands. So she drank it.

Chang'e floated up, up, up to the moon. She would live forever. She would also be separated from her husband for all time.

The archer was sad when he found out. He missed his wife so much. He made her favorite cakes and picked her favorite fruit. He put them on an **altar** and prayed to her. He didn't want her to be lonely on the moon.

Soon, the whole village did the same. They worshiped Chang'e as the Moon Goddess. They prayed to her every year on the day the moon was at its brightest. They asked her for love and peace. They asked for a good harvest for their crops.

Today, the Mid-Autumn Festival
is a time to get together with family.
It is also a time to be thankful for
the harvest.

WHEN IS THE MID-AUTUMN FESTIVAL CELEBRATED?

Some people in the world use a **lunar calendar**. It follows the **phases** of the moon. On this calendar, a year has 12 months. Each month has 29 or 30 days. There are 354 or 355 days in a year.

The symbols of the lunar calendar

JANUARY
2   9   18   25

FEBRUARY
1   8   16   24

MARCH
2   10   18   25

APRIL
1   9   16   23   30

MAY
9   16   22   30

JUNE
7   14   21   29

JULY
7   13   20   28

AUGUST
5   12   19   27

SEPTEMPER
3   10   18   26

OCTOBER
3   9   17   25

NOVEMBER
1   8   16   24   30

DECEMBER
8   16   23   30

NEW MOON   FIRST QUARTER   FULL MOON   LAST QUARTER

A lunar calendar shows the different phases of the moon.

Autumn takes place during the seventh, eighth, and ninth months of this calendar. The Mid-Autumn Festival is celebrated on the 15th day of the eighth month. The full moon is believed to be at its brightest around this time. It looks rounder and more beautiful than the rest of the year.

On other calendars, the date of the Mid-Autumn Festival changes every year. It usually falls around the month of September. But it can be as late as early October.

WHERE IS THE MID-AUTUMN FESTIVAL CELEBRATED?

A Mid-Autumn Festival celebration in Chinatown in San Francisco, California

In China, the Mid-Autumn Festival has been celebrated for more than 3,000 years. Today, it is a three-day holiday. It is also observed outside China. Chinese people who live in Southeast Asia celebrate.

The Mid-Autumn Festival has also become popular in the United States. Large cities host celebrations. There are carnivals with lanterns and special performances of Chinese **operas**.

Other Asian cultures celebrate too. In Japan, this holiday is called Tsukimi. The name means "moon viewing." It is a time to admire the harvest moon. The festival spread to this country 1,000 years ago.

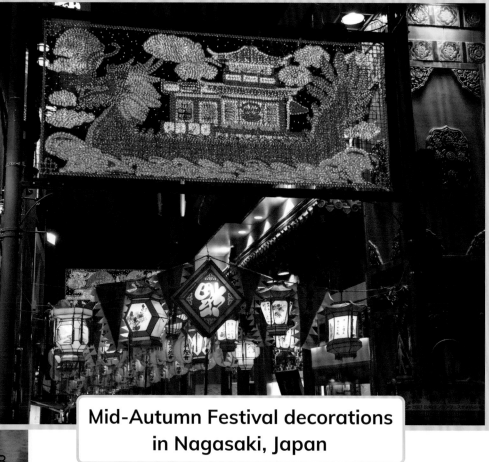

Mid-Autumn Festival decorations in Nagasaki, Japan

People wear traditional dresses in Seoul, South Korea.

In South Korea, the festival is called Chuseok. The name means "autumn evening." It is one of the country's biggest holidays. It is a three-day celebration.

In Vietnam, the holiday is called Tết Trung Thu. It is also known as the Children's Festival. There is a different legend about the moon. It says a man hung onto a magical tree as it floated to the moon. Children carry lanterns to help him find his way home.

The holiday is also a time for family. For farmers, autumn marks the end of farm work. Parents have more time to spend with their children. The multiday celebration is a happy time.

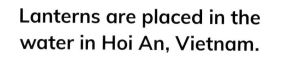

Lanterns are placed in the
water in Hoi An, Vietnam.

HOW DO PEOPLE CELEBRATE?

During the Mid-Autumn Festival, families gather for dinner. It is a happy time to be with loved ones. People eat watermelon and other fruits.

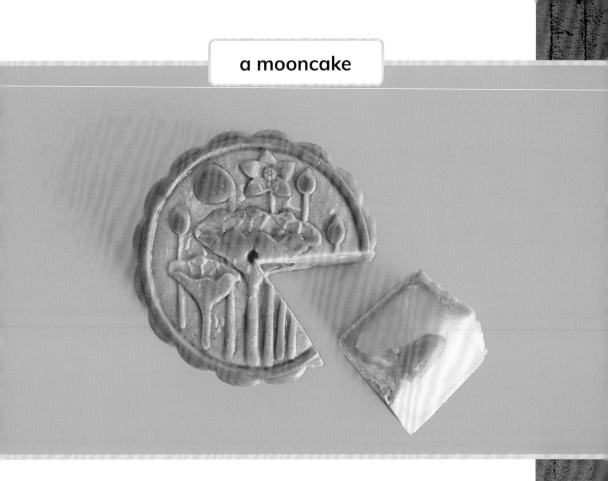

a mooncake

Mooncakes are also popular. These sweet treats are made of bean paste wrapped in a soft dough crust. Some mooncakes have a whole egg yolk in the middle.

After dinner, families go outside. They admire the full moon. Round paper lanterns are hung in trees or on houses. They are lit with candles or small bulbs.

Children often carry smaller lanterns in a **parade** through neighborhoods. Some lanterns are shaped like animals such as horses or dragons. Others are round or shaped like boats.

Lanterns light up the night during the Mid-Autumn Festival in Singapore.

In Singapore and other countries, giant lanterns are **displayed** in parks. They can be as big as a house! Families visit and admire the beautiful decorations.

In Vietnam, parents buy lanterns, snacks, and funny masks for children. Everyone gathers to spend time with family. They play games and share a meal.

Masks for sale in Vietnam

In many countries, there are lion and dragon dances. Dancers wear bright costumes that look like these animals. They perform **acrobatics** and dance to loud music.

The Mid-Autumn Festival is a fun time for the whole family.

People dress up to celebrate the Mid-Autumn Festival in Vietnam.

dragon dancers

GLOSSARY

acrobatics (ak-ruh-BAT-iks)—movements borrowed from gymnastics, such as handstands, flips, and forward rolls

altar (AWL-tuhr)—a platform or table used as a center of worship

archer (AR-chuhr)—a person who shoots at targets with a bow and arrow

display (dih-SPLEY)—to put something in plain sight

legend (LEJ-uhnd)—a story handed down from earlier times; legends are often based on fact, but they are not entirely true

lunar calendar (LOO-nur KAL-uhn-dur)—a calendar that follows the cycles of the moon traveling around Earth

opera (OP-ur-uh)—a play in which the words are sung

parade (puh-RADE)—a line of people, bands, cars, and floats that travels through a town; parades celebrate special events and holidays

phase (FEYZ)—a stage; the moon's phases are the shapes that it appears to take during a month

potion (POH-shun)—a mixture of liquids thought to have magical effects

READ MORE

Cho, Tina. *Korean Celebrations: Festivals, Holidays, and Traditions.* Rutland, VT: Tuttle Publishing, 2019

Qiu, Yobe. *Our Moon Festival: Celebrating the Moon Festival in Asian Communities.* New York: Yobe Qiu Publishing, 2022.

INTERNET SITES

China Highlights: Mid-Autumn Festival for Kids
chinahighlights.com/festivals/mid-autumn-festival-for-kids.htm

Globe Trottin' Kids: Discover the Mid-Autumn Moon Festival
globetrottinkids.com/discover-the-mid-autumn-moon-festival/

Moon Festival for Kids
china-family-adventure.com/moon-festival.html

INDEX

ABOUT THE AUTHOR

photo by C.H. Ang

Ailynn Collins has written many books for children, including stories about aliens and monsters, science and nature, and the past and future. These are her favorite subjects. She was a teacher for many years and mentors kids who love to write stories of their own. Ailynn lives outside Seattle, Washington, with her family and five dogs. When she's not writing, she enjoys participating in dog shows and dog sports.